Contents

CAKES AND COOKIES

DESSERTS

BASIC RECIPES

NEVER-FAIL KIDDIE TREATS

Popular prakashan

www.popularprakashan.com

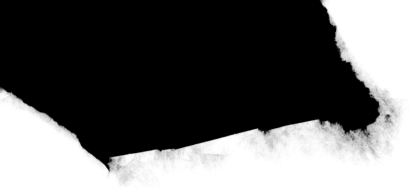

Published by
Harsha Bhatkal for
POPULAR PRAKASHAN PVT. LTD.
301, Mahalaxmi Chambers
22, Bhulabhai Desai Road
Mumbai – 400 026
www.popularprakashan.com

© 2012 FOODFOOD
First Published 2012

(4439)
ISBN: 978-81-7991-691-9

Design: Anjali Sawant
Food Styling & Photography: FOODFOOD

Printed in India by
Sap Print Solutions Pvt. Ltd.
Mumbai - 400 013

"There is no love sincerer than the love of food," wrote the famed satirist and playwright George Bernard Shaw. Perhaps the only love sincerer than food is the love of a mother. And what could be more precious and sincere than the food cooked by a loving mother?

That basically is the philosophy behind Mummy Ka Magic.

*M*ummy Ka Magic is a collection of recipes designed to help hapless mums everywhere deal with the cantankerous, disorderly, obstinate, irrational, tantrum-throwing and idiosyncratic gastronomic fussiness that kids often display at a young age. It provides the answer to every mother's dilemma of what to cook, demonstrating simple recipes that with a little imagination and lots of love, can magically transform a boring dish into a captivating work of culinary art.

*A*ired on FOODFOOD, the most gastronomically loaded food lifestyle and entertainment concept available across TV, mobile, publishing, web, and other media, FOODFOOD is a 360 degree brand in the world of food, and Mummy Ka Magic in a book format is its latest offering.

*T*he efficacy of Mummy Ka Magic is evident by the number of diehard fans the show has collected in such a short period. Yet it is not just about cooking for kids. Mummy Ka Magic is for everyone who savours and relishes food.

*T*his book is for those who love the show and those who missed the show - a keepsake that hopefully will be treasured as much for its contents as its ability to inspire mothers like you to create your own magic in your kitchen.

*H*appy cooking and bon appétit!

 is India's first food and food lifestyle media brand, the brainchild of renowned Master Chef Sanjeev Kapoor.

Targeted at anyone with a passion for food, FOODFOOD, the TV channel was launched on 24 January 2011, and since then has diversified into online and mobile formats, DVDs and cookbooks.

FOODFOOD makes food and cooking fun, easy, joyful and stress free. The channel features various instructional shows, lifestyle shows, food contests, interactive game shows, travelogues to food heavens and more. The shows are hosted by some of the most renowned and experienced chefs and TV personalities adding flavour to the programming on offer.

Some of the most popular shows include:

Sanjeev Kapoor's Kitchen

Master Chef Sanjeev Kapoor shows us what to cook and how. Every day, join Sanjeev Kapoor as he cooks up some of the most interesting, simple and tasty dishes. From starters to desserts, the show features his signature dishes and much more.

Teatime With Chef Rakesh Sethi

Chef Rakesh Sethi makes innovative and easy dishes that are perfect with *chai*. From Indian to fusion, these delicious and nutritious snacks are simple to make and a delight to have on your household menu!

Turban Tadka

The very entertaining Chef Harpal Singh Sokhi treats viewers to the true art of Punjabi cooking. He loves to cook true *desi* style where all that matters is the authentic taste of these everyday Punjabi classics!

Tune in to FOODFOOD for more such shows and indulge your passion for food….

Breakfast

Vermicelli Idli

1 tablespoon oil

1 teaspoon mustard seeds

8 -10 curry leaves

¼ teaspoon asafoetida (*hing*)

1 onion, finely chopped

1½ teaspoons finely
chopped ginger

1 teaspoon chopped
green chillies

2 cups vermicelli, roasted
or unroasted

½ cup boiled green peas

½ cup chopped carrot

½ cup chopped cabbage

2 cups buttermilk

Salt to taste

2 pinches black
pepper powder

1 tablespoon coriander
leaves, finely chopped

8-10 cashew nuts, roasted

To serve
Coconut Chutney (page 102)

*H*eat a *kadai* or wok; add the oil.

*A*dd the mustard seeds, curry leaves, asafoetida, onion, ginger, green chillies, and fry for a few minutes. Add the vermicelli, peas, carrot and cabbage, and mix well.

*A*dd the buttermilk, salt, pepper powder, chopped coriander and cashew nuts and stir. Remove from heat and allow to cool for 10-12 minutes.

*P*our the mixture into greased *idli* moulds and steam for 15-20 minutes. Unmould onto individual plates.

*S*erve hot with coconut chutney.

Serves 4-6

Chocolate-covered Doughnuts

225 grams refined flour (*maida*) + for dusting

2 teaspoons baking powder

85 grams butter

25 grams caster sugar

1 egg

Milk, as required

Oil for deep-frying

125 grams milk chocolate OR dark chocolate

To decorate

Chocolate vermicelli or multi-coloured sprinkles

Sift the flour and baking powder together into a bowl. In a separate bowl, beat the butter and caster sugar till light and fluffy.

Add the egg and move the beater in one direction only. Fold in the flour and mix gently. Add milk as required, to give the mixture the consistency of a soft dough.

Dust a work surface with same flour, and roll out the dough ¾-inch thick. With the help of a doughnut cutter (or with two round cookie cutters of different sizes), cut out doughnut shapes. Dust the cutter with flour to avoid sticking.

Heat the oil in a *kadai* and deep-fry the doughnuts on a low heat till golden brown. Drain on absorbent paper.

For the chocolate covering, melt the chocolate in a double boiler or in a heatproof bowl over a pan of simmering water. Dip one side of each fried doughnut into the melted chocolate and place on a platter, chocolate side up. Sprinkle some chocolate vermicelli or colourful sprinkles on top to decorate.

Leave till the chocolate sets and the doughnuts cool to room temperature.

Serve or store in an airtight container.

Makes 16

Vegetable Frittata

1 tablespoon oil

4 tablespoons sliced mushrooms

2 tablespoons boiled green peas

3 tablespoons chopped carrot

3-4 cherry tomatoes

3-4 boiled potatoes, sliced

6-7 eggs

1 teaspoon salt

1 teaspoon black pepper powder

To serve

Tomato sauce

*H*eat the oil in a large frying pan; add the sliced mushrooms, boiled peas, carrot, cherry tomatoes and sliced potatoes, and fry for a few minutes. In a bowl, add eggs, salt and pepper and beat till fluffy.

*P*our the egg mixture into the pan with the vegetables, cover it with a lid and cook on low heat for a few minutes.

*R*emove the cover, flip the frittata over and cook for 4-5 minutes till both sides are cooked or till the centre is cooked. Transfer to a plate, cut into wedges and serve warm with tomato sauce.

Serves 4

Oats with Soft Eggs

1 cup milk

1 tablespoon sugar or honey

½ cup oats

½ teaspoon salt

1 teaspoon honey

2 tablespoons chopped almonds

1½ tablespoons golden raisins

1 tablespoon black raisins

1½ tablespoons tutti frutti

2 soft-boiled eggs, cut into pieces

*P*ut the milk, ½ cup water, sugar, oats and salt into a pan and bring to a boil. Reduce heat and simmer for a few minutes or till the mixture starts to thicken.

*A*dd the honey. Reserve a few almonds, raisins, black raisins and tutti frutti for decoration, and add the rest to the pan and mix well.

*T*ransfer the mixture to two serving bowls. Add the soft-boiled eggs and mix with a fork. Serve warm, garnished with the reserved dried fruit.

Serves 2

Spanish Layered Eggs

9 eggs

Salt to taste

¼ teaspoon black pepper powder + to taste

3 tablespoons butter

1-2 onions, chopped

2 tablespoons chopped red capsicum

2 tablespoons chopped green capsicum

2 tablespoons chopped yellow capsicum

3-4 mushrooms, sliced

1 tomato, chopped

2 teaspoons oil

50 grams drained (hung) yogurt

100 grams cheese spread

To serve

Bread rolls

Butter

*B*eat the eggs and add salt and black pepper to taste.

*I*n a frying pan, melt 1 tablespoon butter; add the onion, red, green and yellow capsicums, mushrooms and tomato, and sauté for 30 seconds. Set aside.

*F*or each omelette, heat ½ teaspoon butter and ½ teaspoon oil in a frying pan on a low heat. Pour in one-third of the beaten egg, stirring continuously.

*W*hile the eggs are still soft, spread one-third of the sautéed vegetables on top. Cook, on low heat till the omelette puffs up. Transfer to a plate.

*I*n a bowl, mix the drained yogurt and the cheese spread. Stir in the salt and pepper powder to taste.

*O*n a serving platter, arrange alternate layers of omelette and yogurt-cheese spread mixture, ending with a layer of yogurt-cheese spread mixture.

*S*erve with bread rolls and butter.

Serves 4-6

Fruity Cereal Squares

1 cup oats
2 cups chocolate flakes
2 cups cornflakes
1 cup chocolate chips
2 tablespoons honey
1½ cups chocolate sauce
1 cup finely chopped apple
1 cup chopped strawberries
Butter for greasing

Combine all the ingredients, except the apple and strawberries, in a bowl.

Add the chopped apple and strawberries and mix well. Pour the mixture into a greased 8 x 8-inch square cake tin.

Place in a refrigerator to chill for 4 hours. Remove, cut into squares and serve.

Makes 16 squares

Pink Wink Sandwiches

1 cup finely shredded
red cabbage

½ cup boiled and
chopped beetroot

1 cup roughly chopped
cottage cheese (*paneer*)

2 tablespoons drained
(hung) yogurt

½ teaspoon black
pepper powder

1 teaspoon sugar

Salt to taste

2 tablespoons butter

4 bread slices

To serve

Shredded lettuce leaves

Tomato ketchup

French fries

For the filling, in a bowl, mix together the cabbage, beetroot, cottage cheese, drained yogurt, pepper powder, sugar, and salt to taste.

Spread butter on both sides of the bread slices. Spread some filling on one slice, cover it with another slice to make a sandwich.

Place in a sandwich toaster and toast over a gas flame.

Cut into triangles and serve hot with lettuce, tomato ketchup and French fries.

Makes 4 sandwiches

Saturn Eggs

2 bread slices

1 tablespoon butter

1 tablespoon finely chopped red capsicum

1 tablespoon finely chopped green capsicum

1 tablespoon finely chopped yellow capsicum

2 eggs

To garnish
2 coriander sprigs

*C*ut the bread slices into rounds with a cookie cutter and apply some butter on both sides.

*I*n a bowl, mix together red, green and yellow capsicums.

*H*eat a frying pan; add the remaining butter and toast the bread slices. Break an egg on top of each round slice, and sprinkle the colourful chopped capsicum on the egg white around the yolk.

*C*ook the eggs on one side only on low heat till the whites are set.

*T*o cook the yolks, place the pan under a salamander, or grill for 2 minutes.

*T*ransfer to a serving plate and serve hot, garnished with coriander sprigs.

Serves 2

Wholewheat Banana Yogurt Pancakes

For pancakes

1½ cups wholewheat
flour (*atta*)

2 teaspoons baking powder

1 teaspoon vanilla essence

2 eggs

½ cup yogurt

¾ cup milk, or
as required

3 tablespoons sugar

½ teaspoon salt

2 tablespoons butter or oil
for greasing

To decorate

2-3 bananas, peeled
and sliced

3-4 strawberries, halved

Whipped cream, as required

To serve

A few sliced bananas

A few strawberries

2 tablespoons honey
(optional)

2 tablespoons whipped cream

*M*ix all ingredients together, except the butter or oil, in a bowl and make a smooth batter.

*G*rease a non-stick pan with the butter or oil and heat it till moderately hot.

*P*our a ladleful of the batter and spread to make a thin pancake. Cook the pancake on both sides till brown. Make more pancakes till the batter is used up.

*J*ust before serving, decorate each pancake with banana slices to make a smile, 2 halved strawberries for the eyes and pipe some whipped cream for the nose.

*S*erve warm with bananas, strawberries, honey and whipped cream.

Serves 4

Top: Wholewheat Banana Yogurt Pancakes
Bottom: Cheesy Dosa Triangles (page 18)

Cheesy Dosa Triangles

½ cup rice flour

½ cup wholewheat flour (*atta*)

½ cup refined flour (*maida*)

½ cup semolina

Salt to taste

Oil, as required

Stuffing

2 teaspoons oil

1 teaspoon mustard seeds

6-8 curry leaves

¼ teaspoon turmeric powder

3-4 boiled potatoes, peeled and diced

Salt to taste

1 cup grated processed cheese

1 tablespoon coriander leaves, chopped

To serve

Any south Indian chutney

*I*n a bowl, mix together rice flour, wholewheat flour, refined flour, semolina, salt and enough water to make a smooth batter. Set aside to ferment for 30-45 minutes.

*F*or the stuffing, heat the oil in a *kadai*; add the mustard seeds. When the seeds splutter add the curry leaves, turmeric powder, potatoes, and salt and toss to mix. Gently mash the potatoes with the back of the ladle and mix well.

*H*eat a griddle or a *dosa tawa* and pour a little oil on it. Pour a ladleful of the batter and spread with the back of the ladle into a thin round pancake. Drizzle some oil and fry till golden brown and crisp.

*F*lip the *dosa* over, cook for a few seconds and transfer to a clean chopping board. Place some of the prepared filling in the centre of the *dosa* lengthways.

*T*op with grated cheese and chopped coriander. Roll up the *dosa*. Cut into small triangles and serve with any south Indian chutney.

Serves 4

Vegetable Pancakes

1 cup refined flour (*maida*)

½ teaspoon baking powder

1 egg, beaten

½ teaspoon salt

2 tablespoons
chopped spinach

2 tablespoons
chopped carrot

2 tablespoons
chopped broccoli

1 tablespoon
chopped coriander

Oil for frying

To serve
Green Chutney (page 102)

*M*ix together refined flour, baking powder, egg and salt in a bowl. Add sufficient water to make a moderately thick batter.

*A*dd the chopped spinach, carrot, broccoli and coriander, and mix well.

*H*eat a little oil in a frying pan; pour a ladleful of batter onto it and spread to make a pancake. When the underside is golden, flip the pancake and fry till golden brown. Transfer to a plate.

*M*ake the rest of the pancakes in the same way. Serve with green chutney.

Serves 2-3

Apple Sauce Toasties with Tofu

1 teaspoon lemon juice

1 apple, finely chopped

1 tablespoon butter

4 teaspoons sugar

3 tablespoons fresh cream

4 teaspoons finely chopped tofu

2 tablespoons chopped apricots

4 slices wholewheat bread

Butter, as required

2 tablespoons peanut butter

*A*dd the lemon juice to the chopped apples to prevent discolouration.

*T*o make the apple sauce, in a pan, heat butter and sauté the apples till they soften and start changing colour. Add sugar and cook till sugar melts. Add fresh cream and mix well. Add the chopped tofu and apricots.

*C*ut the bread slices into round and heart shapes with cookie cutters. Spread butter on both sides and toast them in a hot frying pan.

*S*pread peanut butter on one side of the toasted slices. Spread the apple sauce on top and serve.

Makes 4 toasties

Beverages and Soups

Triple Flair

½ pineapple, chopped
4-5 kiwi fruit, chopped
1 cup chopped strawberries

To decorate
1 sprig of mint

*P*urée each fruit separately in a blender and pour into jugs. In a tall glass, pour pineapple purée to fill one-third of the glass.

*W*ith the help of a spoon pour kiwi purée on top till the glass is two-third full.

*F*inally, fill the glass with strawberry purée. Decorate with mint leaves. Serve chilled.

Serves 2

Creamy Floats

8-9 crushed chocolate
cream biscuits
1½ cups vanilla ice cream
2 bananas, peeled
and chopped
1 cup strawberry chunks
¼ cup milk
1 teaspoon cocoa powder
¼ tablespoon vanilla essence
1 tablespoon chocolate sauce

To decorate
½ teaspoon cocoa powder

*C*rush 6-7 chocolate cream biscuits in a blender. Reserve 1 scoop of vanilla ice cream and a few slices of banana and add the rest to the blender with the strawberry chunks, milk, cocoa powder and vanilla essence. Blend till smooth.

*L*ine a tall glass with chocolate sauce. Crush the remaining biscuits and place a little at the base of the glass. Add the reserved scoop of vanilla ice cream.

*P*our the blended drink into the glass. As the ice cream rises and floats, decorate with the rest of the crushed biscuits, banana slices and cocoa powder. Serve chilled.

Serves 2-3

Almond Honey Milk

1 litre milk
10-12 blanched almonds
2 tablespoons sugar
2 tablespoons honey
1 cup desiccated coconut
½ cup German Caramel
(see below)
1 teaspoon chocolate chips
2 tablespoon rose syrup

*B*ring the milk to a boil in a pan.

*G*rind blanched almonds, sugar and honey to a fine paste. Add the paste to the milk and mix well. Remove from the heat and leave to cool.

*I*n a bowl, mix together the desiccated coconut and German caramel to make a dough. Divide into equal portions and shape into small balls (*laddu*).

*S*tick 2 chocolate chips on the balls to form eyes. Set aside.

*D*ivide the almond-honey milk into 2 bowls. Add the rose syrup to one bowl and mix well.

*D*ecorate some small bottles. Pour the plain almond-honey milk into half the bottles and the rose-flavoured almond-honey milk into the remaining bottles.

*P*lace one *laddu* each on the mouth of the bottle and serve.

Note: To make German caramel, melt ¼ cup brown sugar in a pan and add 1 tablespoon butter and a pinch of cinnamon powder. Remove from the heat; cool and use as required.

Serves 4

Chocolate Nut Swirl

2 cups whole milk

1 cup chocolate-
hazelnut spread

1 cup crushed ice

To decorate

1 tablespoon chocolate
flakes (optional)

In a pan, heat 1 cup milk and chocolate-hazelnut spread, reserving some to decorate, and cook, stirring, till the spread melts.

Transfer to a bowl, and add the remaining milk and allow to cool.

Process the mixture in a blender with the crushed ice.

Using a long-handled spoon (parfait spoon) line the inside of a tall glass with the chocolate-hazelnut spread.

Pour the blended mixture into the glass and serve, decorated with the chocolate flakes.

Serves 2

Orange Soy Milk Smoothie

2 cups soy milk, chilled

1 cup fresh orange
juice, chilled

2 tablespoons sugar

To decorate

1 tablespoon orange jam
or marmalade

Orange slices or

Crushed ice or

1 scoop vanilla ice cream

Blend together the soy milk, orange juice and sugar in a blender.

Decorate the inside of a tall glass with orange marmalade. Pour the smoothie into it. Garnish with an orange slice and serve.

Alternatively, add crushed ice or decorate with one scoop of vanilla ice cream.

Serves 2

Right: Almond Honey Milk (page 23)
Left: Orange Soy Milk Smoothie

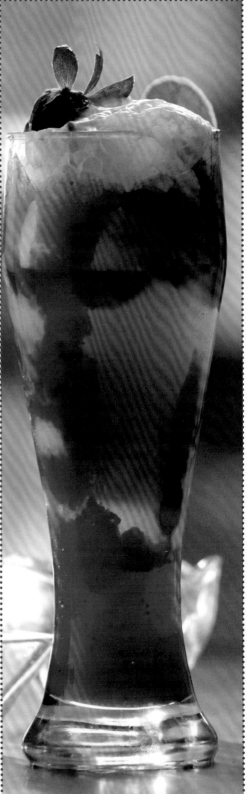

Choco-Banana Shake

2 large bananas,
sliced roughly

1¾ cups milk, chilled

2 tablespoons drinking
chocolate powder OR cocoa

1 tablespoon sugar

1 tablespoon chocolate sauce

To decorate

¼ cup whipped cream

1 banana, sliced

¼ cup glazed red cherries

*I*n a blender, combine bananas, milk, drinking chocolate powder and sugar and blend until smooth.

*L*ine the insides of a tall glass with chocolate sauce and pour the chocolate shake into it.

*P*our the whipped cream into a piping bag with a star nozzle and pipe rosettes on the milkshake. Decorate with sliced banana and glazed red cherries on satay sticks. Serve.

Note: Alternatively, serve the milkshake decorated with a scoop of chocolate ice cream.

Serves 2

Berry Punch

1 tablespoon strawberry jam

2 tablespoons
strawberry crush

2 scoops strawberry
ice cream

6 strawberries, diced

150 ml aerated lemon drink

To decorate

1 strawberry, sliced
into a fan

1 lemon wedge

A sprig of mint

*L*ine the insides of a tall glass with strawberry jam; add strawberry crush, the ice cream and diced strawberries.

*P*our lemon drink into the glass.

*D*ecorate with the strawberry fan, a lemon wedge and sprig of mint. Insert a stirrer and serve.

Serves 1

Left: Choco-Banana Shake
Right: Berry Punch

Cold Watermelon and Pineapple Soup

1 cup chopped pineapple

2 cups watermelon juice

1 teaspoon lemon juice

1 teaspoon honey

2 tablespoons pineapple squash

1 tablespoon chopped pineapple + to serve

A few watermelon balls to decorate + to serve

*P*rocess the pineapple, watermelon juice, lemon juice, honey and pineapple squash in a blender.

*P*lace a few pineapple pieces and watermelon balls in a soup bowl. Pour the blended juice over it.

*S*erve chilled with watermelon balls and pineapple pieces.

Note: *Scoop out watermelon balls with a Parisienne scoop or melon baller.*

Serves 2

Hot Dog Soup

2 teaspoons oil

2 teaspoons finely chopped garlic

3 tablespoons chopped spring onion

½ cup chopped French beans

2 tablespoons diced red capsicum

2 tablespoons diced yellow capsicum

2½ cups Chicken Stock (page 103) or water

1 chicken stock cube

Salt to taste

¼ teaspoon black pepper powder

2-3 chicken sausages, sliced

To garnish

1 tomato, diced

1 tablespoon finely chopped basil

*I*n a pan, heat oil. Add the garlic and sauté for a few seconds.

*A*dd the spring onion, French beans and red and yellow capsicums, and cook for 2-3 minutes.

*A*dd the stock or water and bring to a boil. Add the stock cube, salt and pepper powder.

*A*dd the sliced chicken sausages and cook for 2-3 minutes. Add the diced tomato and basil leaves and serve hot.

Serves 2

Pumpkin and Corn Soup

2 tablespoons + 1 teaspoon butter

1 teaspoon oil

1 onion, chopped

350 grams pumpkin, chopped

200 grams boiled corn kernels

Salt to taste

½ teaspoon black pepper powder

1½ cups Vegetable Stock (page 103)

½ cup milk

2 tablespoons cream

To garnish

Whipped cream

*I*n a *kadai*, heat 2 tablespoons butter and the oil. Add the onion and sauté till golden brown.

*A*dd the pumpkin and 150 grams boiled corn, and cook for 5 minutes. Add salt and pepper to taste.

*A*dd vegetable stock and bring to a boil; lower the heat and cook for 20 minutes. Remove from heat and set aside to cool.

*I*n a separate pan, add 1 teaspoon butter, the remaining boiled corn, salt and pepper and cook on high heat until corn turns golden.

*P*urée the pumpkin mixture in a blender; strain into another pan. Add milk and check the consistency.

*B*ring to a boil, lower the heat and simmer for 2-3 minutes, stirring continuously. Check the seasoning. Stir in the cream. Ladle into bowls and garnish with the seasoned corn and whipped cream.

Serves 3-4

Tofu Noodle Soup

2 tablespoons oil

1 teaspoon finely
chopped garlic

2 tablespoons chopped
shallots

½ teaspoon finely
chopped ginger

1 teaspoon finely chopped
red and green chillies

4-5 mushrooms, sliced

2-inch piece carrot, cut
into thin strips

2 tablespoons peeled,
seeded, and chopped tomato

2 tablespoons diced
tofu (bean curd)

2 tablespoons shredded
cabbage

80 -100 grams boiled noodles

3-4 cups Vegetable Stock
(page 103)

Salt to taste

½ teaspoon black
pepper powder

1 vegetable stock cube

To garnish

1 tablespoon chopped spring
onion greens

1 tablespoon chopped
coriander

*H*eat the oil in a *kadai* and sauté the garlic. Add the shallots and stir-fry. Add the ginger, red and green chillies and fry.

*A*dd sliced mushrooms, carrot, tomato, tofu, shredded cabbage, boiled noodles and vegetable stock.

*B*ring to a boil and cook for 5 minutes. Add salt, pepper and the stock cube.

*L*adle the soup into bowls, garnish with spring onion greens and coriander, and serve hot.

Serves 4

Tomato Soup with a Twist

350 grams tomatoes

1 tablespoon olive oil

10-15 garlic cloves

10-15 basil leaves

Salt to taste

¼ teaspoon black pepper powder + to taste

½ cup tomato purée

2-3 cups Vegetable Stock (page 103) or water

1 potato, boiled and puréed

To garnish

2 tablespoons cream (optional)

¼ cup croûtons

A few basil leaves

Remove the eyes of the tomatoes and make criss-cross slits on the other end. Blanch the tomatoes by plunging them into boiling water for 1 minute. Remove the tomatoes and place them in a bowl of crushed ice and cold water.

Peel the tomatoes and cut them into halves. Remove the seeds by squeezing the tomatoes.

Grease a baking tray with olive oil and place the tomato halves on it. Place a garlic clove and basil leaf on each tomato half. Sprinkle salt and the pepper powder and roast in a preheated oven at 170°C/325°F/ Gas Mark 3, for 10 minutes. Remove from the oven and set aside to cool.

Place the tomatoes in a blender and blend with a little water. Transfer the puréed tomatoes to a pan and add the tomato purée; add a little water or vegetable stock.

Add the salt, sugar and pepper powder and simmer for 5 minutes. Check and correct the consistency by adding the puréed potato. Strain the soup once again into a separate pan and heat it.

Ladle into individual bowls and serve hot, garnished with cream, croûtons and a basil leaf.

Serves 4

Chicken and Cheese Soup

2 tablespoons oil

2-3 cloves garlic, chopped

1 onion, chopped

1 teaspoon roasted cumin seeds, powdered

1 tablespoon refined flour (*maida*)

½ cup boneless chicken, chopped

1 cup Chicken Stock (page 103)

½ cup black-eyed beans, boiled

2 tablespoons chopped red capsicum

2 tablespoons chopped green capsicum

1 tablespoon chopped yellow capsicum

To garnish

1 teaspoon lime juice

½ cup grated Mozzarella cheese

1 teaspoon chopped parsley

In a large pan, heat oil and sauté the garlic and onion. Add the roasted cumin powder and flour; stir and cook for a minute.

Add the chicken and chicken stock and bring to a boil. Simmer till the chicken is cooked and the moisture has almost evaporated.

Add the black-eyed beans and cook for another 2-3 minutes. The mixture should be semi-dry.

Add the capsicums and mix; cook for a minute. Remove from heat.

Transfer to bowls, sprinkle with lime juice, garnish with grated cheese and parsley, and serve hot.

Note: For a vegetarian version, replace the chicken with cubed potatoes.

Serves 2

Snacks

Crispy Fried Chicken

½ litre buttermilk

1 teaspoon salt + to taste

½ teaspoon black pepper powder

500 grams boneless chicken, cut into chunks

200 grams breadcrumbs

100 grams cornflakes

2 eggs

100 grams refined flour

Oil for deep-frying

To serve

Tomato sauce

*I*n a bowl, combine the buttermilk, 1 teaspoon salt and pepper powder.

*A*dd the boneless chicken, mix well and leave to marinate for at least 45 minutes.

*C*ombine the breadcrumbs and cornflakes in a shallow bowl.

*B*eat the eggs, add salt and mix. Set aside.

*R*oll each piece of marinated chicken in the flour, and then place it back into the buttermilk mixture.

*C*oat once again with the flour, dip into the beaten egg mixture and then roll in the breadcrumb and cornflake mixture.

*H*eat the oil in a *kadai* and deep-fry the chicken on low heat until crisp and golden brown. Serve hot with tomato sauce.

Serves 4

Fish and Mango Wrap

250 grams sole fish, cut into medium pieces

1 unripe green mango, finely chopped

Salt to taste

2 tablespoons oil

6-7 curry leaves

2-3 green chillies, chopped

1 tablespoon fresh coriander

For paste

½ cup grated coconut

1 finely chopped onion

2-3 crushed garlic cloves

1 teaspoon finely chopped ginger

1 teaspoon red chilli powder

½ teaspoon turmeric powder

For salad

½ cucumber, chopped

1 tomato, seeded and chopped

1 onion, chopped

Juice of 1 lemon

1 teaspoon black pepper powder

Salt to taste

To serve

2-3 *roti*

Coriander sprigs

Lemon wedges

*T*o make the paste, grind the coconut, onion, garlic, ginger, chilli powder and turmeric powder.

*T*ransfer the paste into a bowl; add the fish, mango and salt, and mix well. Marinate for 30 minutes.

*H*eat the oil in a pan; add the curry leaves and green chillies, and marinated fish and mango.

*C*ook on low heat tossing gently taking care not to break the fish.

*C*ook till the fish is done and all the moisture has evaporated.

*A*dd the chopped coriander and mix. Set aside.

*F*or the salad, mix together the cucumber, tomato, onion, lemon juice, pepper powder and salt.

*T*o serve, heat the *roti*, spread a spoonful of the fish mixture on each *roti* and top with some salad. Roll up the *roti* or fold it in half.

*S*erve warm, garnished with coriander sprigs and lemon wedge.

Makes 2-3 wraps

Nutri Nugget Burgers

4 sesame burger buns
3 tablespoons butter
4 lettuce leaves
4 cheese slices
4 tomato slices
4 cucumber slices

For burger patties
200 grams soya granules
1 medium boiled
potato, mashed
¼ cup shelled green peas
½ teaspoon red chilli powder
1 teaspoon chopped
coriander
Salt to taste
½ cup fresh breadcrumbs
Oil for shallow-frying

To serve
Tomato ketchup
Potato wafers

For the burger patties, soak the soya granules in warm water for 5 minutes.

Squeeze out the water and combine with the mashed potato, peas, chilli powder, chopped coriander, salt, and breadcrumbs in a bowl. Knead the mixture well and shape into 4 round patties.

Heat the oil in a pan and shallow-fry the patties until golden brown.

Cut the sesame bun in half and spread butter on both halves. Place a lettuce leaf, fried patty, a slice each of cheese, tomato and cucumber one on top of the other.

Cover with the other half of the bun and serve with tomato ketchup and potato wafers.

Makes 4 burgers

Mini Tuna Melts

1 cup tinned tuna, flaked

½ cup cold cooked
mushroom soup

1 tablespoon chopped
gherkins

¼ cup finely chopped celery

2 tablespoons finely
chopped onion

1 teaspoon finely chopped
fresh coriander

6 slices processed cheese

12 slices toasted
French bread

*I*n a large bowl, mix together the tuna, mushroom soup, chopped gherkins, celery, onion and coriander.

*C*ut the cheese slices the same size as the French bread slices. Spread 1 tablespoon tuna mixture on each slice of bread and place a cut processed cheese slice on top.

*G*ently and loosely wrap each piece in aluminium foil. Place on a baking tray and heat in a preheated oven at 170°C/325°F/Gas Mark 3, for 10-15 minutes. Unwrap and serve warm.

Note: For a vegetarian version, replace the fish with soya mince (granules).

Makes 12 melts

Nachos and Beans

Nachos

100 grams wholewheat flour

1 tablespoon butter

½ teaspoon baking powder

½ teaspoon onion seeds

Salt to taste

½ teaspoon black
pepper powder

1 tablespoon yogurt

Salsa

¼ cup soaked boiled
kidney beans

2 tablespoons boiled
corn kernels

1 tomato, chopped

2 tablespoons tomato sauce

1 teaspoon lemon juice

Salt to taste

To serve

2 tablespoons grated cheese

Sour cream

For the nachos, combine the flour and the butter in a bowl, and mix well. Add the baking powder, onion seeds, salt, pepper powder and yogurt, and knead into a dough. Rest the dough, covered, for 10-15 minutes.

Preheat the oven to 180°C/350°F/Gas Mark 4.

Roll out the dough into a ¼-inch thick round and cut into small triangular shapes. Prick with a fork to prevent the nachos from puffing up during baking. Arrange the nachos on a greased baking tray and bake for 10-15 minutes.

Remove from the oven and leave to cool.

For the salsa, mix together the kidney beans, corn, tomato, tomato sauce, lemon juice and salt in a bowl.

Spoon the salsa onto the baked nachos and sprinkle grated cheese on top. Serve at once with sour cream on the side.

Note: You can use readymade nachos for this recipe.

Serves 2

Chicken Cutlets

1 cup finely chopped cooked chicken

1 cup grated boiled potatoes

1 finely chopped onion

1 tablespoon finely chopped gherkin

1 tablespoon finely chopped coriander

1 egg, beaten

½ teaspoon black pepper powder

2-3 tablespoons breadcrumbs, or as required

2-3 teaspoons oil for shallow-frying

Coriander sauce

1½ cups milk

1 tablespoon butter

1 tablespoon refined flour (*maida*)

1 tablespoon finely chopped coriander

Salt to taste

¼ teaspoon black pepper powder

½ teaspoon lime juice

1 tablespoon cream

*I*n a bowl, combine cooked chicken, potatoes, onion, gherkin, chopped coriander, egg and pepper and mix well. Add the breadcrumbs if required. Shape the mixture into round patties.

*H*eat the oil in a griddle or pan and shallow-fry the patties until crisp and golden brown on both sides. Arrange in a serving plate.

*T*o make the coriander sauce, bring milk to a boil in a pan. In another pan, melt butter, add flour and cook for a minute, stirring, without colouring it.

*P*our in the boiled milk whisking continuously and cook till it thickens. Add finely chopped coriander, salt, pepper powder and lime juice, and mix well. Stir in the cream and check consistency.

*S*erve chicken cutlets with the coriander sauce.

Serves 3-4

Vegetable Cheesecake

2 tablespoons butter
+ for greasing

1 tablespoon oil

1 cup chopped onion

1 tablespoon chopped garlic

1 cup chopped carrot

2 cups grated bottle
gourd (*lauki*)

3 tablespoons refined
flour (*maida*)

1 tablespoon finely
chopped coriander

Salt to taste

¼ teaspoon black
pepper powder

½ tablespoon dried oregano

1 tablespoon lemon juice

1 cup grated mozzarella
cheese

½ cup grated processed
cheese + 2 tablespoons
for sprinkling

4 eggs

Breadcrumbs, as required

To garnish

Tomato wedges

Coriander sprigs

*I*n a frying pan, heat butter and oil and sauté the chopped onion till golden brown. Add the garlic, carrot, bottle gourd, refined flour, chopped coriander, salt, pepper powder, oregano, and lemon juice and mix well and cook for a minute.

*I*n a separate bowl, mix together the mozzarella cheese, reserving some for garnishing, processed cheese and eggs, and beat until light and fluffy. Add the sautéed vegetables.

*G*rease a 6-inch round springform pan or a quiche dish with butter and sprinkle with breadcrumbs. Pour the vegetable mixture into the pan, and sprinkle a little cheese on top.

*B*ake in a preheated oven at 190°C/375°F/Gas Mark 5, for 20 minutes or till the mixture is cooked. Remove and set aside to cool. Cut into wedges and serve warm or cold, garnished with tomato wedges and coriander sprigs.

Serves 4

Stuffed Cucumber and Tomato

1 tablespoon drained
(hung) yogurt

1 tablespoon cream

Salt to taste

Black pepper powder
to taste

1 tablespoon chopped
walnuts + for garnishing

1 tablespoon chopped olives

1 tablespoon chopped
capsicum

1 tablespoon finely
chopped coriander

1 tablespoon lemon juice

1 cucumber

1 tomato

To garnish
1 sprig of coriander

Black pepper powder

For the stuffing, mix together yogurt and cream, salt, pepper powder, walnuts, olives, capsicum, and coriander in a bowl. Mix well and add lemon juice.

Peel a cucumber and cut it in half lengthways. Scoop out the centre to make a cup. Fill with the prepared filling. Garnish with walnuts.

Cut the tomato in half and scoop out the centre to make a cup. Fill with the mixture. Place in the middle of the prepared cucumbers.

Serve garnished with the coriander sprig and pepper powder.

Serves 2

Tuna Canapés

1 cup flaked tinned tuna

1 cup crushed cornflakes

2 celery stalks, crushed

4 tablespoons Mayonnaise
(page 103)

2 tablespoons grated
cheddar cheese

Salt to taste

½ teaspoon black
pepper powder

½ teaspoon dried oregano

½ teaspoon red chilli flakes

15 canapé cases

To garnish

Finely chopped celery

Grated cheese

*P*lace the tuna in a bowl. Add the crushed cornflakes, celery stalks, mayonnaise and grated cheese. Mix well and mash chunks if any.

*A*dd the salt, pepper powder, oregano and chilli flakes and mix well. Fill the canapé cases with the mixture.

*S*prinkle with celery and cheese.

Makes 15 canapés

Soya Paneer Samose

For pastry

2 cups refined flour (*maida*)

¼ cup semolina

1 teaspoon carom
seeds (*ajwain*)

2 tablespoons pure ghee

Salt to taste

Oil for deep-frying

For filling

1 tablespoon oil

½ cup finely chopped onion

1 teaspoon ginger paste

½ cup chopped tomatoes

1 cup soya granules, soaked
and drained

1 teaspoon turmeric powder

1 teaspoon *garam masala*

1 teaspoon chilli powder

½ teaspoon dried mango
powder (*amchur*)

½ cup roughly chopped
cottage cheese (*paneer*)

Salt to taste

To serve

Green Chutney (page 102) or
Tomato sauce

*F*or the pastry, mix together in a bowl, the flour, semolina, carom seeds, ghee, salt and 1 cup water and mix well to make a dough. Cover with a damp cloth and set aside.

*F*or the filling, heat 1 tablespoon oil in a pan; add the onion and sauté till golden brown. Add ginger and tomatoes and cook for 5-6 minutes.

*A*dd the soya granules, turmeric powder, *garam masala*, chilli powder, dried mango powder, cottage cheese and salt to taste, and mix well.

*D*ivide the dough into walnut-sized balls. Roll each portion into very thin rounds. Cut the rounds in half and shape each half into a cone.

*F*ill the cones with the mixture. Moisten the edges with a little water and press the edges together. Make impressions with a fork along the edges to give it a design and seal the edges.

*H*eat oil in a wok and deep-fry the *samose* till crisp and golden brown. Serve hot with a chutney or sauce.

Serves 4

Top: Soya Paneer Samose
Bottom: Chicken and Apple Sandwich (page 48)

Chicken and Apple Sandwich

1 cup chopped cooked chicken, finely chopped

1-2 tablespoons finely chopped celery

½ cup chopped apple

Salt to taste

1-2 tablespoons Mayonnaise (page 103)

½ teaspoon lemon juice

12 bread slices, toasted

100 grams butter

6 iceberg lettuce leaves

To make each face

1 black olive

1 apple

3-inch sliced celery stalks, as required

1 processed cheese slice

To serve

Wafer

French fries

*M*ix together the chicken, celery, apple, salt, mayonnaise and lemon juice in a bowl.

*F*or each sandwich, cut 2 toasted bread slices into 4-inch rounds with a cookie cutter. Spread butter. Cut a lettuce leaf into 4-inch round with the cookie cutter.

*P*lace the lettuce leaf on a bread slice and spread the chicken mixture over it.

*C*over with the other slice of bread. With the help of the toothpicks insert 2 celery pieces into the sandwich, one on each side to make legs. Make 5 more sandwiches. Set aside.

*T*o make the face, cut an olive into half for eyes, and with the help of a toothpick insert it into the apple. Use sliced celery to make the antennae. Cut the cheese slice into a smile for the caterpillar.

*A*rrange the sandwiches behind the apple to look like a caterpillar. Serve with wafers and French fries.

Makes 6 sandwiches

Corn and Capsicum Calzone

1 tablespoon dry yeast

2 tablespoons caster sugar

1 cup refined flour (*maida*)

1 teaspoon salt

3 teaspoons oil

5-6 garlic cloves, crushed

1 chopped capsicum

3 tablespoons boiled
corn kernels

½ teaspoon ground
black pepper

3 tablespoons grated
mozzarella cheese

1 egg, beaten

To serve
Tomato sauce

*I*n a bowl, mix together yeast and caster sugar with your fingertips. Set aside for 5-10 minutes.

*T*o make the dough, in a bowl, combine the flour, salt, 1 teaspoon oil and yeast mixture and mix well. Leave to rise for 10-15 minutes.

*F*or the stuffing, heat 2 teaspoons oil in a pan. Add crushed garlic and chopped capsicum and sauté for a few seconds. Add the boiled corn, pepper and mozzarella cheese, and cook till the cheese melts. Set aside to cool.

*D*ivide the dough into 4 parts. Shape into balls and roll out into circles.

*F*or each calzone, place a quarter of the stuffing on one half, moisten the edges with water and cover with the other half, pressing down to seal the edges (like *gujiya*). Brush with beaten egg and place on a baking tray.

*B*ake in a preheated oven at 200°C/400°F/Gas Mark 6, for 20-25 minutes. Serve with tomato sauce.

Makes 4 calzone

Chicken and Pineapple Sandwich

¼ cup finely chopped
pineapple

1 cup shredded,
boiled chicken

¼ cup Mayonnaise (page 103)

Salt to taste

2 pinches black
pepper powder

1 tablespoon butter, softened

2 large bread slices

2 lettuce leaves

To serve

Potato wafers or French fries

Tomato sauce

In a bowl, combine the pineapple and shredded chicken. Add the mayonnaise, salt and pepper and mix well.

Butter the bread slices and place a lettuce leaf on each slice.

Spread the chicken-pineapple mixture on top of the lettuce on one slice and cover with the other slice, buttered side down.

Remove the crusts, cut into 2 triangles and serve with wafers or French fries and tomato sauce.

Makes 2 sandwiches

Cheese and Bean Burger

2 burger buns

2 tablespoons butter

For filling

2 teaspoons pure ghee

1 onion, finely chopped

1 green chilli, chopped

1 tablespoon chopped
red capsicum

1 tablespoon chopped
yellow capsicum

1 tablespoon chopped
green capsicum

1 cup tinned baked beans

½ cup cooked rice

Salt to taste

½ teaspoon black
pepper powder

2 tablespoons tomato sauce

2 cheese slices

To serve

French fries

Slice the buns horizontally into 2 and hollow them out with a cookie cutter. Spread the butter on the bun halves.

For the filling, melt the ghee in a pan; add the onion and sauté till golden brown.

Add the green chilli, red, yellow and green capsicum and baked beans and cook for 2-3 minutes. Add the rice, salt, pepper powder and tomato sauce, and cook for 4-5 minutes.

Fill the hollowed out buns with the mixture and top with a slice of cheese. Cover with the top half of the bun and serve hot with French fries.

Makes 2 burgers

Cheese Fondue

2 cups milk

2 tablespoons toasted breadcrumbs

½ cup grated mozzarella cheese

1 tablespoon tomato sauce

1 tablespoon Parmesan cheese

1 teaspoon chilli flakes

1 teaspoon dried oregano

To serve
Pita bread

Bring the milk to a boil in a pan. Add the breadcrumbs, mozzarella cheese, tomato sauce, Parmesan cheese, chilli flakes and oregano, and mix well.

Cook till the mixture thickens. Pour into a fondue pot.

Cut pita bread into pieces and serve.

Wholewheat Vegetable Pizzas

For pizza base

2 cups wholewheat flour (*atta*)

5 grams dry yeast, soaked in lukewarm water

1 teaspoon salt

1 teaspoon sugar

2 tablespoons olive oil

For topping

200 grams pizza sauce

150 grams mozzarella cheese, grated

4 tomato slices

2 black olive slices, stoned

30 grams tomato sauce

*I*n a bowl, mix wheat flour, yeast mixture, salt and sugar, and sufficient water to make a soft and smooth dough. Add the oil and knead again.

*C*over the dough with a piece of wet muslin and allow it to rest for 15-20 minutes or till it ferments and doubles in size.

*P*ress the dough lightly and divide it into 2 equal portions.

*R*oll out each portion into a ¼-inch thick, 10-inch round and prick it with a fork.

*S*pread the pizza sauce over the pizza base and sprinkle the grated cheese on top. Make a smiley face on the pizza with two tomato slices for the eyes.

*B*ake in a preheated oven at 200°C/400°F/Gas Mark 6, for 10 minutes or till the cheese melts. Take care not to over bake the pizza to prevent the tomato slices from wilting.

*R*emove from the oven. Cut an olive into half, and place in the middle of the tomato for eyeballs. Drizzle tomato sauce in the shape of a smile. Serve hot.

Makes 2 pizzas

Mini Chicken Pie

1 cup refined flour (*maida*)

6 tablespoons butter

Salt to taste

1 egg, beaten

For filling

1 tablespoon butter

1 onion, finely chopped

¼ cup chopped celery

2 tablespoons chopped
mushrooms

1 cup chopped,
boiled chicken

½ cup shelled green peas

¼ cup chopped capsicum

2 cups Chicken Stock
(page 103)

Salt to taste

½ teaspoon black
pepper powder

2 tablespoons cream

In a bowl, mix together the flour, butter and salt. Add 5 tablespoons chilled water, and knead to make a dough. Cover the dough and set aside.

For the filling, heat the butter in a pan and sauté the finely chopped onion. Add the celery and mushroom and cook for a few minutes.

Add chicken, green peas, reserving a few for garnishing, capsicum, chicken stock, salt, and pepper powder. Stir and cook for 5-6 minutes. Stir in the cream.

Divide the dough into 2 parts. Roll out one portion of the dough and line a fish-shaped mould with it. Add the cooked chicken mixture.

Roll out the remaining dough and cover the filling, sealing the edges. Prick the dough with a fork. Brush with the egg.

Bake in a preheated oven at 180°C/350°F/Gas Mark 4, for 30-35 minutes. Remove from the oven and cool for 10 minutes.

Unmould and place a green pea for the eye of the fish and serve.

Makes 1 pie

Pesto 'n' Tomato Pinwheels

250 grams refined
flour (*maida*)

½ teaspoon baking powder

1 teaspoon sugar

3 tablespoons soft butter

1 egg, lightly beaten

¾ cup milk + for brushing

½ cup tomato sauce
(approx.)

3 cheese cubes, grated

For coriander pesto

100 grams coriander leaves

1 tablespoon crushed garlic

2 tablespoons
crushed walnuts

1½ tablespoons olive oil

4 tablespoons grated
Parmesan or processed
cheese

To make the pesto, place coriander leaves, garlic, walnuts and 1 tablespoon olive oil in a blender and process until smooth. Gradually add the remaining oil. Transfer to a small bowl and mix in the cheese.

For the pastry, sift the flour and baking powder together into a bowl. Mix in the sugar. Rub in the butter, using your fingertips, until the mixture resembles fine breadcrumbs.

Make a well in the centre of the flour mixture and add the egg and milk. Mix into a soft dough and add more milk if necessary. Rest the dough for 10-15 minutes. Divide the dough in half.

Dust some flour on a flat surface. Roll out each half into a ½-inch thick rectangle. On one half, spread tomato sauce, and on the other spread the coriander pesto. Roll both up like a Swiss roll. Wrap in cling film and place in the refrigerator for 10-15 minutes.

Preheat the oven to 180°C/350°F/Gas Mark 4. Cut the rolls in round slices. Brush with milk and sprinkle grated cheese on top. Place on a greased baking tray and bake in the preheated oven for 20-25 minutes till crisp and golden. Serve hot.

Serves 4-6

Fried Idli

5-6 *idli*, chopped

Oil for deep-frying

4 tablespoons pomegranate seeds (*anardana*)

Salt to taste

1 teaspoon *chaat masala*

1 teaspoon dried mango powder (*amchur*)

1 teaspoon chutney powder (*molagai podi*) + to serve

½ teaspoon red chilli powder

10-12 fried curry leaves

*H*eat the oil in a pan, and deep-fry the chopped *idli* till crisp and golden brown. Drain on absorbent paper.

*T*ransfer to a bowl. Add the pomegranate seeds, salt, *chaat masala*, dried mango powder, chutney powder, chilli powder and fried curry leaves and mix well.

*T*ransfer to a serving bowl and serve warm with more chutney powder or chutney.

Serves 3-4

Main Dishes

Vegetable Lasagne

1 tablespoon olive oil

2 teaspoons finely
chopped garlic

1 large onion, diced

1 medium brinjal, chopped

1 yellow capsicum, chopped

1 red capsicum, chopped

1 zucchini, chopped

2 cups chopped, skinless and
seeded tomatoes

Salt to taste

½ teaspoon black
pepper powder

1 tablespoon finely
chopped basil

10 lasagne sheets, boiled

6-8 tablespoons
mozzarella cheese

For sauce

40 grams butter

2 tablespoons refined
flour (*maida*)

2 cups hot milk

¼ teaspoon grated nutmeg

2-3 tablespoons grated
Parmesan cheese

Salt to taste

¼ teaspoon black
pepper powder

To serve

Lettuce salad with lemon
dressing or

Garlic bread

*H*eat the olive oil in a pan; add the garlic and onion, and sauté till golden brown. Add the brinjal, yellow and red capsicums and zucchini and cook till all the vegetables are tender.

*A*dd the tomatoes, stir to mix and cook till soft and pulpy. Add the salt, pepper powder and chopped basil and remove from the heat.

*T*o make the sauce, heat the butter in another pan and add the flour. Sauté lightly making sure that the flour does not change colour. Add the boiling hot milk, stirring continuously till smooth. Lower the heat and cook for 2 minutes or the mixture thickens to the consistency of a sauce. Add the grated nutmeg, Parmesan cheese, salt, and pepper powder and mix well. Remove from heat and keep warm.

*I*n an 8-inch oval or rectangular baking dish, spread 1 tablespoon sauce; and spread the cooked lasagne sheets to cover the base of the dish.

*S*pread ⅓ of the vegetable mixture. Pour some of the sauce and sprinkle mozzarella cheese. Repeat the process twice and top with the sauce and plenty of cheese.

*B*ake in a preheated oven at 180°C/350°F/Gas Mark 4, for 25-30 minutes, till the top is golden brown.

*S*erve hot with lettuce salad and lemon dressing or with garlic bread.

Serves 4

Vegetable Bouquet

2 tablespoons butter

1 teaspoon chopped garlic

1 onion, chopped

4 bread slices, cut into
small cubes

2 cups prepared mixed
vegetable soup

2 tablespoons tomato purée

100 grams boiled corn

50 grams chopped carrot

50 grams French beans

Salt to taste

½ teaspoon black
pepper powder

¼ teaspoon red chilli powder

2 tablespoons tomato sauce

¼ cup grated cheese

To serve
Bread rolls

*H*eat the butter in a pan. Add the garlic and onion, and sauté till golden brown. Add the bread cubes and stir-fry for 1-2 minutes.

*A*dd the soup, tomato purée, corn, carrot, French beans, salt, pepper, chilli powder and tomato sauce and cook for 5-10 minutes.

*T*ransfer to an 8-inch rectangular or oval dish, top with grated cheese and place under a hot grill till golden brown on top. Serve with bread rolls.

Serves 4

Curd Rice

1 cup yogurt

3 cups cooked rice

1 teaspoon grated ginger

2-3 green chillies,
finely chopped

1 tablespoon crushed
cashew nuts

1½ teaspoons pomegranate
seeds (*anardana*)

1 tablespoon chopped
coriander

Salt to taste

1 tablespoon oil

½ teaspoon mustard seeds

1 teaspoon skinless split
black gram (*urad dal*)

½ teaspoon split Bengal
gram (*chana dal*)

8-10 curry leaves

*I*n a bowl, mix together the yogurt, cooked rice, ginger and green chillies. Add the crushed cashew nuts.

*R*eserving some pomegranate seeds and chopped coriander for garnishing add the rest along with salt to taste and mix well.

*I*n a pan, heat the oil; add the mustard seeds and fry till they begin to splutter.

*A*dd split black gram, and split Bengal gram, and cook on low heat till golden brown. Add the curry leaves and stir. Pour over the yogurt and rice mixture in the bowl and mix.

*P*our the prepared mixture into a bowl. Just before serving, unmould the bowl onto a serving plate.

*S*erve garnished with the reserved pomegranate seeds and chopped coriander.

Serves 3-4

Farfalle in Tomato Sauce

100 grams farfalle

½ teaspoon salt

½ teaspoon oil

For sauce

5-6 tomatoes

2 tablespoons olive oil

1 cup chopped onions

4-5 garlic cloves, crushed

4 tablespoons chopped
yellow capsicum

Salt to taste

1 teaspoon chilli flakes

1 teaspoon black pepper
powder

1 teaspoon dried oregano

2 tablespoons tomato sauce

1 tablespoon chopped olives

3 tablespoons grated
Parmesan cheese

To garnish

Oregano

Grated Parmesan cheese

Chilli flakes

*B*ring plenty of water to a boil in a large pan; add farfalle, salt and oil, and cook till *al dente* (cooked but firm to the bite). Drain.

*F*or the sauce, blanch the tomatoes in boiling water. Remove the skin and seeds. Roughly chop the blanched tomatoes.

*H*eat the olive oil in a pan; add the onion and garlic and sauté till golden brown.

*A*dd the yellow capsicum, tomatoes, salt, chilli flakes, pepper powder, oregano and tomato sauce and cook for 5-6 minutes. Add the boiled pasta, chopped olives, Parmesan cheese, and mix well.

*T*ransfer to a serving plate and sprinkle with oregano, grated cheese and chilli flakes, and serve hot.

Serves 1-2

Kedgeree

1 tablespoon butter

1 onion, chopped

1 teaspoon curry powder

¼ cup boiled green peas

½ cup tinned tuna, flaked

Salt to taste

2 cups cooked Basmati rice

To decorate

1 onion, sliced and deep-fried till brown

2 green olive slices

Tomato strips

2 sprigs of coriander

*I*n a pan, melt butter over medium heat. Add chopped onion and sauté till translucent. Add the curry powder and cook for half a minute.

*A*dd the boiled peas and tuna; stir to mix. Add the salt, rice and ½ cup water, and cook for 6 minutes. Remove from heat and set aside.

*A*t the base of a greased 8-inch round cake tin, arrange the fried onion at the top end to make hair. Place the olive slices for eyes and the tomato strips for a nose and smiling mouth.

*G*ently ladle the cooked rice mixture into the prepared cake tin and press down firmly. Leave to set for a few minutes.

*T*urn the rice out onto a serving plate and serve warm garnished with the sprigs of coriander.

Serves 2-3

Spaghetti Cake

250 gm spaghetti

1 teaspoon salt + to taste

1 tablespoon oil

4 eggs

3 chopped tomatoes

2 cups finely chopped spinach

1 cup grated processed cheese

3 cups cream

¼ teaspoon black pepper powder

Butter for greasing

To garnish

1 sprig of basil

*B*ring plenty of water to a boil in a large pan; add spaghetti, 1 teaspoon salt and 1 teaspoon oil and cook till *al dente* (cooked but firm to the bite). Drain.

*I*n a bowl, beat eggs and add tomatoes, finely chopped spinach, grated cheese and cream. Mix well.

*A*dd salt and pepper powder. Mix in the strained spaghetti.

*G*rease a 10-inch round loose-bottomed or spring-form baking tin with butter, and pour the mixture into it. Bake in a preheated oven at 180°C/350°F/Gas Mark 4, for 25-30 minutes.

*R*emove from the oven and leave to cool. When still a little warm, release the sides of the cake from tin and unmould carefully.

*T*ransfer to a serving plate, garnish with basil leaves and serve.

Serves 4-6

Potato Gnocchi

3-4 boiled potatoes, mashed

2-3 eggs

Salt to taste

2-3 cups refined flour (*maida*)

1-2 tablespoons butter

1-2 tablespoons grated
Parmesan cheese

1 teaspoon dried oregano

1 teaspoon chopped parsley

To serve

2 slices garlic bread

*F*or the gnocchi, combine mashed potato, eggs, and salt in a bowl. Add enough flour to make a soft dough. Roll small portions of the dough into long cylinders and cut into ½-inch pieces.

*B*ring plenty of water to a boil in a pan; add 1 teaspoon salt and the gnocchi and cook for 2-3 minutes till the gnocchi are cooked and rise to the surface. Remove with a slotted spoon and transfer to another pan.

*A*dd the butter and toss the gnocchi in it. Add salt and sprinkle the Parmesan cheese and oregano on top. Add the chopped parsley and toss.

*S*erve with garlic bread.

Serves 4

Corn and Bean Rice

1 cup half-cooked
Basmati rice

2 large tomatoes, chopped

½ cup corn kernels, boiled

1 cup kidney beans
(*rajma*), boiled

2 green chillies,
finely chopped

Salt to taste

1 teaspoon red chilli powder

1½ cups grated
processed cheese

To decorate

2 tablespoons tomato sauce

1 tablespoon Mayonnaise
(page 103)

1 sprig of coriander

*P*reheat the oven to 200°C/400°F/Gas Mark 6.

*C*ombine the rice, 1¼ cups water, tomatoes, corn, kidney beans, green chillies, salt and chilli powder in a bowl. Mix gently.

*T*ransfer the mixture into a greased baking dish and cover the dish with aluminium foil. Bake in the preheated oven till the rice is cooked but still moist. Remove and set aside to cool.

*S*pread grated cheese at the base of a teddy bear or a flower-shaped ovenproof flexi mould, and add the rice and kidney bean mixture. Loosely cover the mould with an aluminium foil and place on a baking tray.

*B*ake for 10-15 minutes or till the cheese melts. Remove from oven and set aside to cool for 5 minutes. Turn out of the mould, decorate with tomato sauce, mayonnaise and coriander leaves and serve.

Serves 2-3

Chicken and Chickpea Casserole

1 teaspoon oil

1 bay leaf

3 tablespoons finely chopped onion

1 tablespoon chopped garlic

200 grams boneless chicken, diced

1 medium cup diced potatoes

½ medium cup diced carrots, blanched

1 cup Vegetable Stock (page 103)

Salt to taste

¼ teaspoon black pepper powder

½ cup boiled chickpeas

¼ cup boiled broccoli florets

2 tablespoons tomato purée

2 tablespoons cream (optional)

2 tomatoes, blanched, peeled, seeded and diced

4-5 basil leaves

To serve

Bread rolls or
Steamed rice

*H*eat the oil in a pan; add the bay leaf and onion and sauté till the onions turn pink. Add the chopped garlic and fry for 2 minutes.

*A*dd the diced chicken and sauté for 3-4 minutes till the chicken is partially cooked. Add the potatoes, carrot and vegetable stock.

*A*dd salt and pepper and bring to a boil. Lower the heat and simmer till the vegetables are almost tender.

*A*dd the boiled chickpeas and boiled broccoli and cook till vegetables are completely cooked. Add tomato purée and cook for another 2 minutes. Add the cream and mix. Add the diced tomatoes and mix well.

*G*arnish with basil and serve with bread rolls or rice.

Serves 2-3

Cakes and Cookies

Fruit 'n' Oatmeal Cookies

1¼ cups butter, softened

1 cup sugar

1 egg

1¼ teaspoons vanilla essence

1½ cups refined flour (*maida*)

1 teaspoon soda bicarbonate

1 teaspoon salt

½ teaspoon ground cinnamon

½ teaspoon ground nutmeg

3 cups quick cooking oats

1 cup dried fruit and tutti frutti

*P*reheat oven to 170°C/325°F/Gas Mark 3.

*I*n a large bowl, cream together the butter and sugar until light and fluffy. Beat in the egg and vanilla essence.

*S*ift together the flour, soda bicarbonate, salt, cinnamon and nutmeg. Gradually fold into the creamed mixture. Finally, stir in the quick oats and dried fruit and tutti frutti.

*D*rop by rounded spoonfuls onto a baking tray lined with butter paper.

*B*ake for 10 to 12 minutes in the preheated oven. Remove from the oven and set aside to cool and serve.

Serves 6-8

Puppy Dog Cookies

200 grams refined
flour (*maida*)

50 grams icing sugar

125 grams butter

1 teaspoon vanilla essence

1 tablespoon chocolate chips

To decorate

Chocolate chips, as required

¼ cup chocolate cereal

1 tablespoon chocolate
vermicelli

*M*ix together refined flour, icing sugar and butter in a bowl. Add 2 tablespoons cold water and the vanilla essence and knead to make a smooth dough. Rest the dough for 10 minutes.

*M*ake 10-15 small round balls and flatten slightly. Place 3-4 pieces of chocolate chips in the centre of each one. Bring the edges together to enclose the chocolate chips and shape into round cookie.

*P*lace the cookies on a greased baking tray. Shape each cookie into a puppy face by fixing 2 pieces of chocolate cereal as the ears, chocolate vermicelli for the eyes and a chocolate chip for the nose.

*P*lace the baking tray in a preheated oven and bake at 170°C/325°F/Gas Mark 3, for 20-25 minutes. Remove from the oven and set aside to cool.

*S*tore in an air-tight container.

Makes 10-15 cookies

Jam Cookies

1 cup (230 gm) soft butter

⅔ cup sugar

2 eggs

2 cup (260 gm) refined flour
+ for dusting

¼ teaspoon salt

1 pinch nutmeg powder

1 pinch clove powder

1 cup (110 gm)
chopped almonds

½ cup mixed fruit jam

2 tablespoons icing sugar,
for dusting

*B*eat together butter and sugar in a bowl, until the mixture is light and fluffy. Add the eggs one by one and beat again till sugar is completely dissolved.

*I*n a separate bowl, sift together the flour, salt, nutmeg powder, and clove powder.

*F*old the flour mixture into the creamed mixture. Fold in the almonds. Cover the dough with cling wrap and refrigerate for 1 hour.

*P*reheat the oven to 170°C/325°F/Gas Mark 3. Sprinkle some flour on the worktop and roll out the chilled dough to ½-inch (1 cm) thickness. Cut out heart shapes with a heart-shaped cookie cutter. Take a heart-shaped cookie cutter smaller in size than the previous one. Cut half of the heart-shaped cookies with the smaller cookie cutter. Use the cut-out cookies, and knead the tiny heart-shaped cut-outs to make more cookies.

*P*lace the cookies on a butter paper-lined baking tray and bake for 10-12 minutes till golden brown. Remove from the oven and set aside to cool.

*S*pread jam on the whole cookie bases. Dust the cut-out heart-shaped cookies with icing sugar and place on top of the base. Add more jam in the centre if desired.

Makes 18 cookies

Bunny Cupcakes

1½ cups refined flour (*maida*)

1 teaspoons baking powder

1 cup caster sugar

½ cup butter

2 large eggs

1 teaspoons vanilla essence

To decorate

½ cup Chocolate Icing
(page 102)

1 tablespoon almonds

1 tablespoon cherries

2 tablespoons sugar-coated
chocolate

1 tablespoon vermicelli/
noodles, fried and cut into
2-inch pieces

Sift together the refined flour and baking powder.

In a bowl, cream the caster sugar and butter. Add the eggs one by one and vanilla essence and beat till fluffy. Add the flour and mix well to make a thick batter.

Pour the batter into cupcake moulds lined with paper cases and bake in a preheated oven at 180°C/350°F/ Gas Mark 4, for 15-20 minutes. Remove from the oven and leave to cool.

Unmould and spread some chocolate icing on top. To decorate, place 2 almonds on the sides of the cupcakes for the ears, place a cherry for the nose, sugar-coated chocolate for the eyes and for the whiskers use the fried noodles.

Makes 12 cupcakes

Eggless Fudge Brownies

100 grams butter

1 cup powdered sugar

1 cup drained (hung) yogurt

¼ cup chopped walnuts

50 grams grated
dark chocolate

½ cup refined flour (*maida*)

1 teaspoon baking powder

½ cup cocoa powder

1 teaspoon vanilla essence

In a bowl, beat butter and sugar and beat till creamy and fluffy. Add the yogurt and beat well.

Fold in the walnuts, grated chocolate, flour, baking powder, cocoa powder and vanilla essence.

Pour the batter into a greased 8-inch baking tin and bake in a preheated oven at 180°C/350°F/Gas Mark 4, for 40 minutes. Remove from the oven and leave to cool.

Remove from the tin, cut into squares and serve.

Makes 12-16 brownies

Oat Muffins

1 cup refined flour (*maida*)

1 teaspoon baking powder

1 cup caster sugar

¼ cup melted butter

2 eggs

2-3 tablespoons milk

1 teaspoon vanilla essence

¼ cup oats

To decorate

4 tablespoons Glace Icing (page 102)

4 tablespoons Chocolate Icing (page 102)

1 tablespoon star-shaped sugar candies

Sift together the flour and baking powder in a bowl.

In another bowl, mix together caster sugar and butter and beat till light and fluffy. Add the eggs, milk and vanilla essence and beat well.

Add flour and oats and mix well to make a thick batter. Transfer the batter into a piping bag and fill into muffin moulds lined with paper cups.

Bake in a preheated oven at 180°C/350°F/Gas Mark 4, for 15-20 minutes. Remove from the oven and leave to cool.

Decorate with glace and chocolate icing and sugar candies and serve.

Makes 6-8 muffins

Little Flowers

1 cup caster sugar

1 cup butter

5 eggs

1 tablespoon vanilla essence

1 cup refined flour (*maida*)

2 teaspoons baking powder

½ cup oats

½ cup chopped
dried apricots

½ cup finely
chopped walnuts

2 tablespoons
chopped prunes

2 tablespoons
sunflower seeds

2 tablespoons raisins

1 banana, finely chopped

For topping

2 tablespoons butter

2 tablespoons sugar

2 tablespoons chopped
dried apricots

2 tablespoons oats

2 tablespoons
chopped prunes

1 tablespoon
sunflower seeds

2 tablespoons raisins

2 tablespoons finely
chopped walnuts

1 banana, finely chopped

*I*n a bowl, mix together caster sugar and butter and beat till light and fluffy. Add the eggs and vanilla essence and beat well. Sift together the flour and baking powder.

*A*dd the flour, oats, dried apricots, walnuts, prunes, sunflower seeds, raisins and banana. Mix well to make a thick batter.

*P*our the batter into sunflower-shaped moulds and bake in a preheated oven at 180°C/350°F/Gas Mark 4, for 15-20 minutes. Remove from the oven and set aside to cool.

*F*or the topping, heat the butter in a pan and add the sugar. Cook till the sugar caramelises. Add the apricots, oats, prunes, sunflower seeds, raisins, walnuts and banana and mix well.

*T*urn out the 'little flowers' onto a plate. Cover with the topping and serve.

Serves 6-8

Mountain Cake

150 grams refined
flour (*maida*)

1 teaspoon baking powder

2 pinches nutmeg powder

1½ cups caster sugar

1 cup butter

5 eggs

2 tablespoons milk

1 teaspoon vanilla essence

To decorate

200 grams whipped cream

1 tablespoon cocoa powder

*S*ift together flour, baking powder and nutmeg powder in a bowl.

*I*n another bowl, mix together caster sugar and butter and beat till light and fluffy. Add the eggs one by one and beat well.

*A*dd milk, and vanilla essence and beat again. Add the flour mixture and stir to remove all lumps.

*P*reheat oven to 180°C/350°F/Gas Mark 4. Pour the batter into a greased 8-inch baking tin and bake for 15-20 minutes. Remove from the oven and cool. Turn out when cold.

*T*o decorate, spread the whipped cream over the cake. Lift the cream into peaks with a spoon. Sprinkle cocoa powder over the cream through a strainer.

*R*efrigerate and serve chilled.

Makes one 8-inch cake

Monster Cookies

2 cups refined flour (*maida*)

1 teaspoon soda bicarbonate

1 teaspoon salt

¾ cup brown sugar

1 cup butter

¾ cup sugar

2 eggs

1 teaspoon vanilla essence

To decorate

Tutti frutti

¼ cup colourful candy-coated chocolate buttons

*P*reheat oven to 170°C/325°F/Gas Mark 3.

*S*ift together the flour, soda bicarbonate and salt.

*M*ix together brown sugar and butter and beat until light and fluffy. Add the sugar, eggs and vanilla essence and beat till the sugar dissolves. Fold in the flour mixture.

*M*ake 20 small balls from the cookie dough, and place them on a butter paper-lined baking tray. Decorate with tutti frutti and candy-coated chocolate buttons.

*B*ake for 15-20 minutes. Remove from the oven and set aside to cool.

Makes 20 cookies

Choco Blocks

1 cup refined flour (*maida*)

¼ teaspoon soda bicarbonate

½ teaspoon salt

½ cup oats

½ cup brown sugar

½ teaspoon cinnamon powder

½ cup dark chocolate, chopped

¼ cup mixed dried nuts and raisins

½ cup honey

½ cup oil

½ teaspoon vanilla essence

½ cup white chocolate

¼ cup dark chocolate

*P*reheat the oven to 170°C/325°F/Gas Mark 3.

*S*ift together the flour, soda bicarbonate, and salt. Mix together the oats, brown sugar, flour mixture, cinnamon powder, and ½ cup dark chocolate.

*A*dd the dried nuts and raisins, honey, oil and vanilla essence and mix well.

*S*pread the mixture in an 8-inch rectangular baking dish or a greased cake tin, pressing down well. Bake for 25-30 minute, till brown.

*R*emove from the oven and set aside for 10-15 minute to cool.

*I*n the meanwhile, in two separate heat proof bowls, melt white chocolate and dark chocolate using a double boiler.

*T*urn out the baked cereal bar onto a dish with the smooth surface facing up.

*P*our the melted white chocolate over the top to cover the whole surface. Place dollops of melted dark chocolate at intervals on top. Swirl the chocolate in a zigzag motion with the help of a toothpick to get a marbled effect.

*R*efrigerate for an hour till set. Cut into slices or bars and serve.

Makes 16 blocks

Desserts

Chocolate Mice

300 grams eggless
sponge cake

100 ml Sugar Syrup
(page 103)

250 grams dark chocolate,
finely chopped

30 grams almonds, halved

30 grams spaghetti or
noodles, deep-fried

20 grams silver vermicelli

40 grams glazed cherries

In a bowl, crumble the sponge cake and moisten with sugar syrup. Mix to form a dough. Shape small portions into ovals.

Melt the chocolate in a double boiler or in a heatproof bowl over a pan of simmering water.

Dip the cake ovals in the melted chocolate to coat well and leave on a wire rack for excess chocolate to drain.

To make the mice, decorate the chocolate-coated shapes with sliced almonds for the ears, a 3-inch piece of fried spaghetti for the tail, silver vermicelli for the whiskers and a sliced cherry for the nose.

Refrigerate till set and serve chilled.

Serves 4-6

Top: Chocolate Mice
Bottom: Chocolate Spiders (page 88)

Butterscotch Bananas

2 bananas
3 scoops vanilla ice cream
6 glazed cherries
2 tablespoons tutti frutti
2 mint sprigs

For butterscotch sauce
2 tablespoons butter
¼ cup brown sugar
¼ cup milk
¼ teaspoon vanilla essence

Bake bananas with the peel on in a preheated oven at 170°C/325°F/Gas Mark 3, for 5 minutes.

To make the butterscotch sauce, in a pan, heat the butter and brown sugar till the sugar melts.

Add the milk and cook for 3-4 minutes or till the sauce thickens. Remove from the heat and add the vanilla essence. Set aside to cool.

Remove bananas from the oven and peel them. Cut them lengthways and arrange in an oval dish.

Top with scoops of vanilla ice cream and pour the butterscotch sauce on top. Decorate with glazed cherries, tutti frutti, and mint sprigs, and serve.

Serves 2

Chocolate Spiders

1 cup noodles

Oil for deep-frying

1 cup dark chocolate, chopped

¼ cup candy coated chocolate buttons

*H*eat the oil in a *kadai* and deep-fry the noodles. Drain on absorbent paper. Break the noodles into 2-inch long pieces. Set aside.

*M*elt the chocolate in a double boiler or in a heatproof bowl over a pan of simmering water. Set aside to cool.

*A*dd the fried noodles to the melted chocolate and, with the help of a fork and spoon, place portions on a baking tray lined with butter paper to make the body of the spider.

*P*lace chocolate buttons in the centre of the noodles for the spiders' eyes.

*A*rrange a few noodles to make the legs of the spider. Chill in the refrigerator for 15-20 minutes and serve.

Serves 4-6

Stuffed Apple Boats

2 red apples, halved

2 teaspoons lemon juice

1 red apple, finely chopped

4 tablespoons finely chopped dates

½ cup chopped walnuts

4 teaspoons raisins

¼ teaspoon cinnamon powder

2 teaspoons caster sugar

To decorate

4 strawberries

1 teaspoon chocolate vermicelli

*B*rush apples with ½ teaspoon lemon juice.

*H*ollow out the halved apples with a spoon. Apply 1 teaspoon lemon juice on the inside walls of the apple halves.

*C*hop the scooped out apple and mix in the remaining lemon juice and add to the chopped apple. Set aside.

*I*n a bowl, add the finely chopped apples, dates, walnuts, raisins, cinnamon powder and caster sugar, and mix well. Fill the hollowed out apples with the mixture.

*D*ecorate each apple with a strawberry and sprinkle chocolate vermicelli. Serve chilled.

Makes 4 boats

Apple Burfi

4 cups caster sugar

3 cups grated coconut

2 cups peeled and chopped, apple, sprinkled with lemon juice

1 teaspoon ginger juice (optional)

Juice of ½ lemon

1 tablespoon oil, for greasing

To decorate

2 tablespoons pistachios, blanched, peeled and chopped

*P*lace the caster sugar, grated coconut and 1 tablespoon water in a pan and cook on a low heat for 5-6 minutes, till the sugar dissolves.

*A*dd the chopped apple, ginger juice and lemon juice and cook for 8-10 minutes, stirring continuously, till the apples are soft and pulpy.

*S*pread the apple mixture into a 6-inch greased baking tin and leave to set. Press down with a spoon to compact the mixture. Sprinkle with the chopped pistachios.

*P*lace in a refrigerator for 3-4 hours to set. Cut into pieces and serve.

Serves 4-6

Bread Halwa

6-8 white bread slices

3-4 tablespoons butter

1 cup sugar

2 cups milk

3 tablespoons pure ghee

To decorate

8-10 cashew nuts, chopped

2 tablespoons raisins

2 pinches of cardamom powder

1 tablespoon tutti frutti

*S*pread both sides of the bread slices with butter and heat in a pan till toasted on both sides.

*T*o make the sugar syrup, cook 1 cup sugar and 1½ cups water in a pan on low heat till the sugar melts.

*B*ring the milk to a boil in a separate pan. Sauté the cashew nuts in ghee and set aside.

*P*lace the toasted bread in a serving bowl, pour sugar syrup and milk over. Set aside till the bread soaks in all the sugar syrup and milk mixture. Alternatively, stir the bread with the help of a fork till it attains the consistency of *halwa*.

*S*prinkle with the cashew nuts, raisins, cardamom powder and tutti frutti.

*S*erve hot or cold.

Serves 4

Dried Fruit Treats

¼ cup oats

¼ cup cashew nuts, chopped

¼ cup walnuts, chopped

¼ cup almonds, chopped

¼ cup raisins, chopped

¼ cup desiccated coconut + for coating

2 tablespoons honey

For butterscotch sauce

¾ cup sugar

2 tablespoons butter

½ cup milk

*D*ry-roast the oats in a pan.

*I*n a bowl, combine the roasted oats, chopped nuts, raisins and desiccated coconut.

*T*o make the butterscotch sauce, place the sugar in a pan and cook over low heat, stirring continuously. Add the butter and milk and mix well. Cook for a minute and transfer to a bowl.

*P*our the hot butterscotch sauce over the oat mixture; add the honey and mix well. Set aside to cool.

*S*hape the mixture into walnut-sized balls; roll in desiccated coconut and serve.

Serves 4-6

Khajoori Laddu

1 cup finely chopped dates

1 cup finely chopped dried figs (*anjeer*)

½ cup milk powder

2 tablespoons milk

2 tablespoons sugar

1 tablespoon finely chopped pistachios

To decorate

10 almonds, blanched and halved

*I*n a thick-bottomed pan, mix together the dates, figs, milk powder, milk and sugar.

*C*ook over medium heat, stirring, till the mixture turns pinkish and the mixture starts to come together. It may take 10-15 minutes.

*T*ransfer the mixture into a bowl and set aside to cool. Place in a refrigerator to set for 1-2 hours.

*A*dd the pistachios and mix well. Divide into equal portions and shape into walnut-sized *laddu*.

*D*ecorate with almonds and serve.

Serves 4-6

Chocolate Cheesecake Pudding

1 cup white chocolate, grated

½ cup cream cheese

½ cup drained (hung) yogurt

2 tablespoons caster sugar

1 teaspoon cinnamon powder

2-3 cream-filled chocolate cookies, crushed

To decorate

¼ cup heart-shaped sugar candies

Dark chocolate shavings

*M*elt the white chocolate in a double boiler or in a heatproof bowl over a pan of simmering water.

*I*n a separate bowl, combine the cream cheese, drained yogurt, caster sugar, cinnamon powder and the melted white chocolate, and mix well. Beat till light and fluffy.

*P*lace the crushed cookies in a small glass bowl, and pour the white chocolate mixture on top.

*P*lace in a refrigerator to set for 2-3 hours.

*J*ust before serving, remove from the refrigerator; decorate with sugar candies and dark chocolate shavings.

Serves 4

Orange Trifle

½ cup (100 grams) marmalade

10 sponge cake slices

100 ml Sugar Syrup (page 103)

3 tablespoons brown sugar

5-6 orange segments, peeled

1 banana, diced

100 grams grapes, halved

40-50 grams almonds, chopped

For custard

5 egg yolks

3 tbsp caster sugar

2 teaspoons custard powder

4-5 drops vanilla essence

2 cups cream or milk

To decorate

200 grams whipped cream or marmalade

Spread the marmalade on the cake slices and sandwich 2 slices together.

Cut the sandwiches into small pieces and place them in the sugar syrup till they soak in the syrup.

To make the custard, mix together the egg yolks, caster sugar, custard powder and vanilla essence in a pan. Add the cream or boiled milk, cook, stirring continuously, till the sugar dissolves. Remove from heat and set aside to cool.

Heat the brown sugar in another pan till it caramelises. Add the orange segments, coating them well with the caramel.

To assemble the trifle, brush the insides of a glass bowl with some marmalade.

Place the soaked cake cubes in the bowl; top with the banana, grapes, caramelised orange slices, and chopped almonds, reserving a few of each for decoration. Pour the custard over. Refrigerate till set.

Decorate with whipped cream, and the reserved caramelised orange slices, banana and grapes.

Alternatively pipe some marmalade over the top to decorate.

Serves 4-6

Cocoa Pancakes with Cinnamon Sauce

1 cup refined flour (*maida*)

1½ teaspoons baking powder

¼ teaspoon salt

1 teaspoon sugar

1 egg

1-2 tablespoons cocoa powder

1 cup milk

1 teaspoon oil

Cinnamon sauce

½ cup sugar

½ teaspoon cinnamon powder

A pinch of salt

1 teaspoon butter

To decorate

Whipped cream

*S*ift together the flour, baking powder and salt.

*I*n a bowl, combine the flour mixture, sugar, egg, cocoa powder and milk to make a smooth batter.

*T*o make the cinnamon sauce, place the sugar, cinnamon powder, salt and a little water, and cook till thick. Stir in the butter and remove from heat.

*H*eat the oil in a small frying pan, and pour in a ladleful of batter. When bubbles appear on the surface, flip the pancake over. Cook for a few seconds and remove to a plate. Keep warm. Prepare pancakes till all the batter is used up.

*T*o serve, place a pancake and spread a thin layer of cinnamon sauce. Repeat till all the pancakes and the sauce is used up. The pile will resemble a cake.

*D*ecorate the top and the sides with the whipped cream using a piping bag with a star nozzle.

Serves 4

Jello Sail Boats

2 cups prepared orange jelly

2 cups prepared
strawberry jelly

2 cups prepared lime jelly

6 large oranges

Glazed paper, as required

Toothpicks, as required

*P*repare orange, strawberry and lime jelly, by following the instructions on the packet.

*W*ash and cut oranges horizontally in half and remove the insides of the orange.

*F*ill the orange halves with the prepared jelly and place in the refrigerator until the jelly sets completely.

*R*emove from the refrigerator and cut each orange half in half again.

*C*ut triangles out of glazed paper and fix onto a toothpick.

*S*tick the sails into the boats and serve immediately.

Makes 24 boats

Chilled Banana Dessert

150 grams sweetened whipped cream

150 grams chocolate ice cream

2 bananas

In a bowl, combine the whipped cream and chocolate ice cream. Work fast so that the ice cream does not melt.

Slice the bananas diagonally and place 2 halves at the base of a mould. Spoon half the chocolate ice cream mixture on top.

Add the remaining banana halves and top with the rest of the chocolate ice cream mixture.

Refrigerate for 4-5 hours till set. Turn out of the mould and serve.

Serves 2

Beastie Eyes

7- 8 plain biscuits

1 tablespoon butter

1 tablespoon peanut butter

2 teaspoons caster sugar

1 cup chopped dark chocolate

Candy coated chocolate buttons

*I*n a large bowl, crumble the biscuits with your fingers. Add the butter, peanut butter and caster sugar, and mix well.

*W*ith a small ice cream scoop or rounded spoon, scoop out small round balls onto a plate. Shape the balls with moistened fingers if necessary.

*D*ip the scoop into water before scooping out the mixture each time. Refrigerate for 3-4 hours.

*M*elt the chocolate in a double boiler or in a heatproof bowl over a pan of simmering water.

*B*rush the melted dark chocolate over the ball, leaving 2 spaces adjacent to each other uncovered to resemble the white of the eye. Refrigerate for 30 minutes.

*W*ith a little melted chocolate, fix a coloured chocolate button in the centre of each space to resemble the pupil of the eye.

*C*hill and serve.

Serves 2

Basic Recipes

Icings

Chocolate Icing

Heat ½ cup heavy cream in a pan. Remove from heat and add 200 grams finely chopped sweet dark chocolate, and stir until smooth.

Note: For white chocolate frosting, replace the dark chocolate with white chocolate.

Glace Icing

Sift 100 grams icing sugar. Add 1-2 tablespoons water, gradually, and a few drops of food colour if desired, stirring well to mix till you get the desired consistency.

Royal Icing

Place 1 egg white in a bowl and whisk lightly with a wooden spoon. Sift 1 cup icing sugar, gradually add to the bowl and stir well. Mix in a few drops of lemon juice to retain whiteness. Royal icing is ideal for piping designs on iced cakes.

Chutneys, Sauces and Syrup

Coconut Chutney

Grind 1 cup grated coconut, adding very little water, to a thick consistency. Add salt to taste, mix well and transfer to a bowl. Heat 2 tablespoons oil in a pan, add 2 dried red chillies, broken into 3 pieces each, ¼ teaspoon mustard seeds, and ½ teaspoon skinless split black gram. When the seeds start to splutter and the gram turns light brown, add a large pinch of asafoetida and 7-8 curry leaves. Add the seasoning to the ground coconut and cover the bowl immediately to trap the flavours. Mix well and serve.

Green Chutney

Grind together 30 grams mint leaves, 100 grams coriander leaves, 2-3 green chillies and 20 grams peeled unripe mango, to a fine paste. Transfer to a bowl and stir in salt to taste and juice of ½ lemon. Store in a refrigerator.

Eggless Mayonnaise

Whisk together ¼ cup cream, ¼ teaspoon mustard paste, ½ teaspoon lemon juice, ½ teaspoon black pepper powder and salt to taste in a clean dry bowl. Add ¾ cup oil a little by little, whisking continuously, till all the oil is incorporated.

Mayonnaise

Place 1 egg yolk, salt to taste, ¼ teaspoon each white pepper powder, French mustard and sugar and 1 teaspoon vinegar in a clean bowl and mix thoroughly with a whisk. Alternatively, process the mixture in a blender. Add 1 cup of oil, a little at a time, whisking or blending continuously, until all the oil is incorporated. Add 1 teaspoon lemon juice and adjust seasoning. Store in an airtight jar in a refrigerator.

Sugar Syrup

Combine 2 cups water and 1 cup sugar in a pan and bring to a boil. Add 1 tablespoon lemon juice and simmer until sugar has dissolved. Skim off the scum that rises to the surface and discard. Transfer sugar syrup to a bowl and set aside to cool.
Note: For a thinner syrup add 3 cups of water.

Stocks

Chicken Stock

Boil 200 grams chicken bones in water for 5 minutes. Drain and discard water. Boil blanched bones with a roughly chopped carrot, celery stalk, leek, 2-3 parsley stalks, 6-7 black peppercorns, 5-6 cloves, 1 bay leaf and 10 cups of water.
Remove any scum which rises to the surface and replace it with more cold water. Simmer for at least 1 hour. Remove from heat, strain, cool and store in a refrigerator till further use.

Vegetable Stock

Heat ½ tablespoon oil in a pan; add 10-12 black peppercorns and 1 bay leaf, and sauté for a few seconds. Add 2 diced onions, 1 diced carrot, and 1 diced turnip and ¼ cup diced celery and sauté till the onions are translucent. Add 2-2½ litres water and bring to a boil. Simmer for 30-45 minutes. Remove from heat and pass through a piece of muslin. Use as required.

my ka Magic